S0-DFE-607

Barkerville

British Columbia's Heritage of Gold

CHRIS HARRIS

text by Bill Horne

COUNTRY LIGHT PUBLISHING
Discover British Columbia Books™

Designed, edited and typeset by Bill Horne

Printed and bound in China

Canadian Cataloguing in Publication Data

Harris, Chris, 1939-

    Barkerville: British Columbia's heritage of gold

(Discover British Columbia Books)

ISBN 0-9695235-8-0

    1. Barkerville (B.C.) - Pictorial works. I. Title. II. Series.

FC3849.B37H37 1999	971.1'75	C99-900441-7
F1089.5.B37H37 1999		

Care has been taken to match this book's printed colours as closely as possible to the original 35 mm slides. They have not been digitally enhanced or altered.

Cover: The Cornish water wheel rises above Williams Creek.
Back cover: St. Saviour's Church at dawn in January.
Facing page: St. Saviour's Church.

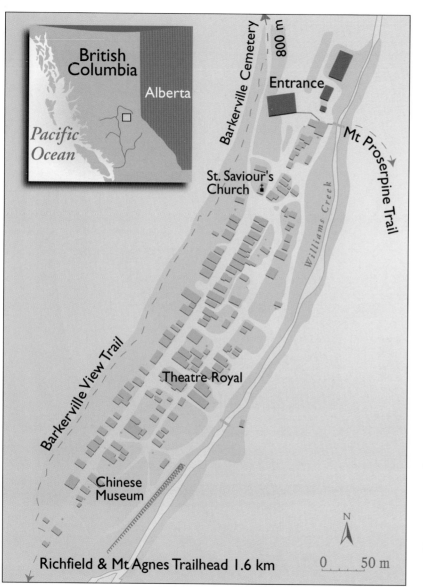

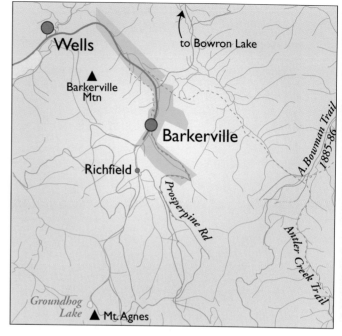

British Columbia
Alberta
Pacific Ocean

Barkerville Cemetery

800 m

Entrance

Mt Proserpine Trail

St. Saviour's Church

Williams Creek

Barkerville View Trail

Theatre Royal

Chinese Museum

N

Richfield & Mt Agnes Trailhead 1.6 km

0   50 m

Wells

Barkerville Mtn

to Bowron Lake

A. Bowman Trail 1885-86

Barkerville

Richfield

Prosperpine Rd

Antler Creek Trail

Groundhog Lake

Mt. Agnes

Above: Barkerville Historic Park.

Left: Barkerville townsite.

Administration buildings

Historic buildings

Hiking, skiing, snowmobiling trails

Park boundary

Barkerville's fire of 1868 destroyed 20 general stores, 18 saloons, eight boarding houses, four shoe stores, four carpentry shops, three barber shops, three butcher shops and two banks, a library, as well as numerous other small businesses and institutions.
Photo P672; clipping P2364.

Dedication

To the miners and fortune seekers of days gone by, and to those who keep the spirit of Barkerville alive today.

Acknowledgements

Special thanks to W.G. Quackenbush, Barkerville Curator, for his painstaking assistance with photographs, source material, and history, Duane Abel, Curatorial Assistant, who helped scan archival photographs, and Faith Moosang, who reviewed the Chinese history and located potential photographs from the Hoy Collection. For additional assistance: at Barkerville, Dianne Lawson, Regional Manager, Northern Interior Region, B.C. Heritage Branch; Robin Sharpe, Manager, Visitor Programs & Communications, Lorne Sisley, Manager, Business Services; Jim Weston at Heritage.

Sheril Mathews, Christine Pilgrim, and Judy Campbell reviewed advance drafts, Marie Nagel proofed copy and Kate Sulis provided additional support. Claire Kujundzic gave constant encouragement and assisted with selection, design, colour and typography. Thanks also to the many other people of Wells and Barkerville who reviewed early drafts and gave suggestions.

The following actors, musicians, models, interpreters and Barkerville business people appear in the book, gave logistical help and made suggestions: *Danette Boucher, Dave Brown, Lynnette Candy, Mark Charnell, Johnson Cheng, Harold Clark, Mark Dawson, Gabe Fourchalk, Larry Fourchalk, Brad Gibson, Jason Griffin, Joseph Jourdain, Alice Jourmel, Oliver Jourmel, Andrea Laurent,* *Sheril Mathews, Jason Mitchell, Rod Nagel, Don Noble, Bettina Schoen, Thomas Schoen, Michael Booth Palmer, Christine Pilgrim, Bob Rae, Scott Rae, Bob Smith, Pat Taylor, Sara Taylor Gibson, Shelley Unger, and Const. Alastair Gray of the RCMP.*

For computer support and imaging: CustomColour, Danny Wong of Cordova Systems, Alan Zisman, Russell Kildal, Gek-Bee Siow, Marc Furney, and Brad Hammerstron of Image House.

Barkerville townsite base map designed by Bill Horne, using base map courtesy of B.C. Heritage. Area map designed by Bill Horne, using base map courtesy of Wells & Area Trails Society and West Fraser Mills.

All black and white archival photos reproduced courtesy of Barkerville Historic Town archives; catalogue numbers are attached for reference.

The creation of the series "Discover British Columbia Books"™ has been greatly assisted by the generous contributions of three corporations. I would like to express my sincere appreciation to Uwe Mummenhoff of Lowepro who supplied me with the most innovative and durable camera carrying equipment. Whether I travel by horse, raft, canoe, plane or foot, Lowepro made the job easier. I would also like to thank Allen Slade of Patagonia for supplying my photo models and myself with the very best in outdoor clothing - be it for rugged wilderness or casual urban wear. Both companies are environmental leaders and share the book series'

vision of preserving our planet's natural heritage. I am also greatly appreciative for the generous supply of film provided by Graham Pask of Kodak Canada. Every image in this book series has been taken with Kodak Elite 100 slide film. Where speed was required, the film was pushed to 200. In my quest for colour, sharpness and contrast, Kodak Elite continually met the challenge.

- Chris Harris

A Mountie chats with a Barkerville visitor on the boardwalk outside the House Hotel Coffee Saloon.

Like the "Never Sweat" shown here, what miners named their claims often gave clues to their origins and aspirations: *Fail-me-not, Dead Broke, Last Chance, Wake-Up-Jake, Pocohontas, California, Glasgow.*

Barkerville's Past and Present

Gold brought miners by the thousands to the Cariboo in the 1860's. By 1864 at the peak of the gold rush that started along the Fraser River, there were 10,000 on Williams Creek, making Barkerville the biggest town west of Chicago and north of San Francisco.

But gold brought more than men, picks and shovels. The Washington Treaty of 1846 had established the boundary at the 49th parallel, but many Americans still wanted to annex British Columbia - now a tantalizing source of gold - and eventually all of Canada. Because of their frustrations with the colonial administration based in New Westminster and later in Victoria, the majority of Cariboo miners favoured confederation. The American

threat simply increased the incentive to establish sovereignty through a Canadian nation stretching from east to west. Thus Cariboo gold hastened the process of confederation and helped bring British Columbia into the new Dominion of Canada.

The miners' conditions were rough: they lived in tents or small one-room cabins, and subsisted on beans and bacon. Most men had little clothing apart from what they wore or could carry. Hard labour, long winters, and swarms of summer mosquitoes wore down their bodies. Hills clearcut for lumber caused flash floods, and most deaths were caused by accidents in mining shafts.

In spite of these conditions, the Cariboo *Sentinel* counted very few arrests and trials, especially compared to the lawlessness of the earlier California gold rush. This was in part due to Judge Begbie and his constabulary's strict and uncompromising British justice. But the miners also realized that their survival in such a harsh, isolated setting depended on mutual aid, so they themselves helped maintain law and order. If there was a distinguishing quality about Cariboo culture, it was honesty and generosity. They may have drank and gambled heavily, but they would never refuse a meal for a hungry traveller.

Diversity helped many endure the boom and bust economy of gold mining. For example, as well as cleaning gold pannings, John Bowron was a librarian and postmaster. Knott was a carpenter and stable keeper, and Lamon's stable in Richfield sold liquor on the side. When one pieman's pies didn't sell, he opened a bath house. Not surprisingly in a region where winter can last eight months, this eclectic kind of economy continues to this day.

After the panning and shafts of the 1860's, hydraulic mining followed, but production never again matched the peak years. Barkerville's population continued to decline until a small influx during the 1930's depression, when the town of Wells grew up nearby, based on underground gold quartz mining. Then it waned again, though the town site never really died.

In 1953, alarmed by the demolition of old historic buildings, resident Fred Ludditt formed the Barkerville Historic and Development Company, and the Wells-Barkerville Centennial Committee followed. Finally in 1958, the B.C. government made Barkerville a historic park and began to renovate the buildings. The plan was never to recreate the town exactly as it was, but to capture its essence. It was an ambitious task.

Pack horses.

P1260

The Hotel de France cost $10,000 to build.

Today Barkerville is the largest historic site in B.C., with buildings and artifacts that represent nearly every decade of its life from the 1860's through to the 1950's. B.C.'s Heritage Branch maintains the site, plans displays, and conducts research, while merchants run shops and restaurants, interpreters guide visitors through the streets, and a theatre company performs musical plays at the Theatre Royal. All dress in period costume and speak of the past in present tense. Those who sing in the streets, hold court, or serve dishes from the Gold Rush, take great pride in their work. Their love for the place is contagious. These are the people who make Barkerville come alive.

The town bustles from May to September when tourists come to pan for gold or explore the shops, theatre and displays. In winter it seems to hibernate, cocooned in the deep snow of the Cariboo. Snowmobilers access alpine trails from the parking lot, while skiers slip quietly through the late 19th and early 20th century streetscapes on their way to Richfield and higher slopes beyond. But funding cuts threaten this precious piece of B.C. history and culture. It is our hope that this book will increase the public's appreciation of Barkerville, so that together, we can ensure it remains a public resource accessible to all, and true to its Cariboo roots.

Clockwise from top left: Dave Perkins, Len Ford, Al Johnson, Ed Owen, Frank Hoffercamp, Joe Hopwood, Eddie Bowron; unidentified man standing at rear. *Staged photo by J.H. Blome circa 1900.*

The Mucho Oro Claim, powered by water from Stout's Gulch. c. 1868.

Romans designed the "Cornish" water wheels for the tin mines of Cornwall. This one operates in Barkerville.

Remains of a stamp mill used to crush ore.

Cajoling an audience of tourists, the "Sheepskin Claim" operators re-enact a scene from history by trying to solicit investors.

Whether the paydirt comes from the surface or from the bottom of a shaft, panning has been used to recover gold.

Tourists join a wedding procession down the main street
of Barkerville.

The main street of Barkerville just after sunrise.

A Mr. Mundy taught just seven pupils at the first school at Stout's Gulch in 1871. Today the Williams Creek Schoolhouse runs classes for visitors of all ages in *Deportment, Decorum and Discipline*, as well as *the Three R's*.

Two of Barkerville's aspiring actors do their laundry on a sunny day.

A dust storm swirls around a stage coach of tourists entering Barkerville.

The Goldfields Bakery sells fresh scones, eccles cakes and, of course, sourdough bread.

An interpreter in period costume brings history to life outside the St. George Hotel.

Making an iron fire poker for sale at the Cameron
& Ames Blacksmith Shop.

The Postmaster sorts the daily mail while a customer addresses
his postcard home.

Taking a break at the Livery & Stables, the main barn for the BX stage coach.

Interior of a reconstructed miner's cabin.

On the boardwalk in Barkerville.

Chinese immigrants played a key role in Barkerville's history. Most originated in the Pearl River delta area of China, and came north to the Cariboo from the California gold rush. As early as 1861, 36 of them held free miner's licenses. Ah Sing was the first recorded as living in Barkerville and by 1867, there were 685 Chinese in addition to the 920 whites.

Some mined or ran laundries and other shops, while others maintained the flumes bringing water from the mountains to the mines. A few built stone terraced gardens on the hill facing Chinatown and Chuk Chung had one in Richfield. The Kwong Lee Company opened a store in Barkerville in 1866 and sold specialties like betel nuts, incense oil, and opium. According to the *Sentinel*, it "suffered the third largest loss of any individual or business in Barkerville" in the great fire.

Chinese miners were persistent and industrious, often successfully reworking gravels abandoned by whites. Yet racial discrimination was common. They were not allowed to vote, and articles in the *Sentinel* denounced their culture and practices. The Chinese Freemasons' society worked to protect their members' interests under these conditions, and organized funerals, banquets and celebrations of the Five Ancestors. Barkerville's Chinese Museum opened in 1997 and honours these pioneers' contributions with displays and documentation.

Many buildings remain in Chinatown at the south end of Barkerville. The Kwong Sang Wing and Kwong Lee Wing Kee operate across from the Lung Duck Tong Restaurant and the Museum.

Working with traditional hand tools, without power, at the Holt & Burgess
Cabinet Shop.

NEW DOMINION DAY

The First Anniversary of the Dominion of Canada
will be celebrated on Wednesday next, July 1st,
at Barkerville, by public competitions in the
Athletic Games and Sports of Canada
and other public amusements.
Several prizes will be awarded to
the successful competitors.
Games to begin at THREE o'clock p.m.
Grand display of FIREWORKS
about ten o'clock p.m. etc.

BY ORDER OF THE COMMITTEE

James Carson   J.O. McKay
Joseph Hough   Richard Wells

Ad recreated from the June 29, 1868 issue
of the Cariboo *Sentinel*.

The greasy pole contest judge shouts encouragement
and waves the prize bottle of whiskey.

Contestants in the annual nail hammering contest try to drive nails into a plank with the least possible number of blows.

The hose carriage races give members of the Williams Creek Fire Brigade a chance to practice their drill and entertain the townfolk.

After the great fire four months earlier, a new Theatre Royal building opened in January, 1869. The theatre operates again today, with historical musicals performed by the resident company.

The Hurdy girls were brought from Germany and Holland. Miners could pay $1 to dance with them, and if they bought drinks, the girls received a percentage. Today the Hurdies and other actors and musicians once again perform on Barkerville's streets and boardwalks.

P757

Tourists can explore the town by stage coach and experience what travel was like in the Gold Rush era when it took four days to travel from Ashcroft to Barkerville.

It's a short trip along the historic Cariboo Waggon Road to Richfield.

P884

Though Barkerville superseded it in size and population, Richfield remained the Cariboo's civil and administrative centre for a long time. Its stately court house, built by I.B. Mason in 1882, replaced the log cabin previously used for 20 years. For the first time in nearly 90 years, a trial took place here in June, 1996. Mr. Justice Parrett of the B.C. Supreme Court presided over this unusual assault case which resulted in an "arresting" of the jury's verdict.

With a height of six foot four and known for his strict rule of law, Judge Matthew Bailie Begbie commanded respect throughout the Cariboo. Today actors re-enact some of the trials he presided over.

Judge Begbie.

Barkerville's main street in February.

A party of skiers heads through Barkerville's Chinatown on their way to Richfield and the alpine areas beyond.

Though the shops are closed in the winter, Barkerville's streets remain open year round.

An accumulated snowfall of 20 feet is not unusual.

Sleigh rides and caroling are part of Barkerville's Victorian Christmas festivities.

St. Saviour's Church on a January afternoon.

Reverend James Reynard, who held his first local services in the Penfold Saloon card room, designed the building and raised most of the construction and operating funds, sacrificing his family's financial needs and his own physical health in the process. He wrote "we live as cheaply as possible. Potatoes on Sundays by way of marking the Christian feast, and a cabbage on Christmas day as a very especial delicacy." Reynard died in 1875 at age 45.

St. Saviour's Church has held services since it opened September 18, 1870, making it the oldest continuously-used church in B.C. It was built by carpenters Bruce & Mann with local pine. In spite of being located on a claim, the church was granted a free title in 1871 and remains on the same site with its original glass, stove, pews and bishop's chair.

The distinctive wooden headboards and picketed graves of the Barkerville cemetery. To this day it has been the final resting place for residents of the area since one of Cariboo John Cameron's workers died and was buried on the hillside. A Cemetery Board now maintains and administers the site according to an architectural plan.

F. J. Barnard's Express hauled mail between Barkerville and Williams Lake twice a week in 1865.

A grizzly bear pelt hangs from the Michael Claim cabin.

Near the stables.

Traces of history abound throughout the townsite.

Cow parsnips and willows encroach on a back street cabin.

Local area residents and visitors carry their home-made lanterns in a procession up Barkerville's main street during Chinese Autumn Moon Festival celebrations.

August rain.

How to Get There • What to Do • Where to Stay

BARKERVILLE

P.O. Box 19, Barkerville B.C. V0K 1B0
250-994-3332
http://www.heritage.gov.bc.ca/

266 Oliver, Williams Lake, B.C. V2G 1M1
1-800-663-5885 fax 250-392-2838
cta@cariboocountry.org

City of Quesnel
405 Barlow, Quesnel, B.C. V2J 2C3
1-800-992-4922
www.city.quesnel.bc.ca

District of Wells
Box 219, Wells, B.C. V0K 2R0
250-994-3330 or 250-994-3422
wells@goldcity.net

1-888-BCFERRY in British Columbia
250-386-3431 in Victoria or long distance
http://www.bcferries.bc.ca/

Recommended Reading

G.P.V. Akrigg and Helen B. Akrigg, British Columbia Chronicle 1847-1871 - Gold and Colonists, Discovery Press, Vancouver, 1977.

Jean Barman, The West Beyond the West - a History of British Columbia, University of Toronto Press, Toronto, 1991.

Isabel M. L. Bescoby, Some Aspects of Society in Cariboo from its discovery until 1871, Masters thesis, UBC, Vancouver, 1932.

Harry Con, Ronald J. Con, Graham Johnson, Edgar Wiekberg, William E. Willmott; edited by Edgar Wickberg, From China to Canada - A History of the Chinese Communities in Canada, McClelland and Stewart, Toronto, 1988. James Doody, The Romance of the Cariboo Proper, Quesnel, 1982.

Perry Kellar, The Chinese in Barkerville, manuscript, Barkerville Historic Town Library, 1980.

David Chuenyan Lai, Chinatowns - Towns Within Cities in Canada, UBC Press, Vancouver, 1988.

Susan M. Lambeth, A Discussion of the Chinatown Component in Barkerville, 1981, Heritage Conservation Branch, Ministry of the Provincial Secretary and Government Services, Victoria, B.C.

Fred Ludditt, Barkerville Days, Mitchell Press, Vancouver, 1969.

Douglas John McCallum, Barkerville Theatre in Context - A Case Study in Our Theatrical Past, MA Thesis, Faculty of Graduate Studies, Department of Theatre, UBC, Vancouver, 1981.

Margaret A. Ormsby, British Columbia - A History, Macmillan of Canada, Vancouver, 1958.

Mark Sachs, Aspects of Chinese Living and Working Spaces in Historical Barkerville, manuscript, Barkerville Historic Town Library, 1982.

Richard Wright, Barkerville Williams Creek, Cariboo - A Gold Rush Experience, Winters Quarter Press, Duncan, B.C., and Friends of Barkerville and Cariboo Goldfields Historical Society, Barkerville, 1993.

Portrait of Billy Barker.

P52

Bill Phinney on the Caledonia Claim 1868.

P1458

COUNTRY LIGHT PUBLISHING

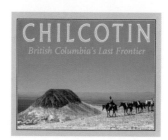

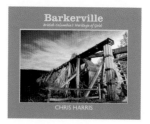

Discover British Columbia Books™

Box 333, 108 Mile Ranch, BC V0K 2Z0
Tel (250) 791-6631 Fax (250) 791-6671

photography@chrisharris.com
www.chrisharris.com